Looking at . . . Pterodactylus

A Pterosaur from the JURASSIC Period

Weekly Reader®
BOOKS

Published by arrangement with Gareth Stevens, Inc.
Newfield Publications is a federally registered trademark
of Newfield Publications, Inc. Weekly Reader is a federally
registered trademark of Weekly Reader Corporation.

Library of Congress Cataloging-in-Publication Data

Coleman, Graham, 1963-
  Looking at-- Pterodactylus/written by Graham Coleman;
illustrated by Tony Gibbons.
    p. cm. -- (The New dinosaur collection)
  Includes index.
  ISBN 0-8368-1143-7
  1. Pterodactylus--Juvenile literature. [1. Pterodactyls.
2. Pterosaurs. 3. Dinosaurs.] I. Gibbons, Tony, ill. II. Title.
III. Series.
QE862.P7C65 1994
567.9'7--dc20   94-16966

This North American edition first published in 1994 by
Gareth Stevens Publishing
1555 North RiverCenter Drive, Suite 201
Milwaukee, Wisconsin 53212 USA

This U.S. edition © 1994 by Gareth Stevens, Inc. Created with original © 1994 by
Quartz Editorial Services, Premier House, 112 Station Road, Edgware HA8 7AQ U.K.

Consultant: Dr. David Norman, Director of the Sedgwick Museum of Geology,
University of Cambridge, England.

Additional artwork by Clare Herronneau.

Printed in the United States of America

Weekly Reader Books Presents

Looking at . . . Pterodactylus

A Pterosaur from the JURASSIC Period

by Graham Coleman

Illustrated by Tony Gibbons

Gareth Stevens Publishing
MILWAUKEE

Contents

Introducing
Pterodactylus

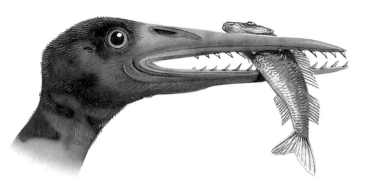

Is it a bird? Is it a dinosaur? No! Watch out, it's a **Pterodactylus** (TER-OH-<u>DAK</u>-TIL-<u>US</u>), soaring in the prehistoric skies!

But although these creatures had a lot in common with dinosaurs, they were a separate group of animals. They were not birds, either. They flew, but they were very different from the birds that lived during prehistoric times and from the birds we know today.

Join us as we take a look at a strange-winged creature that flew over our planet some 150 million years ago, during the Late Jurassic Period.

A flying reptile, **Pterodactylus** lived at the same time as many of the dinosaurs. That's why we have chosen to include it in *The New Dinosaur Collection*.

So **Pterodactylus** was neither a dinosaur nor a bird. It was a pterosaur (<u>TER</u>-OH-<u>SOAR</u>).

What, then, were pterosaurs? What did **Pterodactylus** look like? How did it fly, and what did it eat?

Read on to find out all about these amazing flying creatures.

5

Master of the skies

Imagine living in those parts of the world we now know as England, Germany, France, and Africa when **Pterodactylus** soared the skies. An amazing flying creature is fishing for food.

It had a tail that was a lot shorter than the tails of other pterosaurs, but this was long enough to help **Pterodactylus** keep its balance when in flight.

Pterodactylus looked very different from the flying creatures we know today, and it had sharp teeth!

Some types of **Pterodactylus** were small, about the size of a water bird, such as a gallinule or duck. Others were as large as today's vultures. The smallest Pterodactylus ever discovered was a baby, with a body length not much bigger than a thumbnail.

Scientists believe **Pterodactylus** was covered with soft hairs. Its wings, however, were hairless.

Like all pterosaurs, **Pterodactylus** is likely to have reached adult size quite quickly. It did not continue growing, like reptiles do, throughout its life.

One puzzle about **Pterodactylus** and other pterosaurs is whether they swam or not. Most lived near lakes or seas, where there was plenty of food. But almost all scientists now think that **Pterodactylus** did not swim. Instead, these animals may have dived down to the surface of the water or skimmed along the top to catch fish.

Built for flight

Pterodactylus had quite a long beak with a number of sharp teeth. Its neck was also rather long, but its tail was fairly short. It had light, hollow bones that kept its weight down. This was important because, if it had been too heavy, Pterodactylus would not have been able to get off the ground and soar way up in the sky.

Pterodactylus must have had a fairly large brain to help control its wings. It also had large eye sockets, so it probably had good eyesight. This would have helped it see across long distances as it flew over the landscape below. It needed to spot danger well in advance and to spy prey for its next meals.

Pterodactylus had a body that was well adapted to flight.

Take a look at the three small, clawed fingers that it had at the end of each arm. Now look at its most striking feature – the fourth finger. This was extremely long, and is known as the "wing finger" because it was attached to its wing.

Pterodactylus also had five toes on each leg, but one toe was too small to be of any real use.

It could travel faster and much farther than dinosaurs and, indeed, many other pterosaurs. But it was not designed to move with ease on the ground. However, it could probably have stood on all fours, balancing gingerly, providing there was no strong wind to throw it off balance.

Any damage to **Pterodactylus**'s wings would have made its life very difficult.

After an active day in the skies, **Pterodactylus** would have needed to rest. So, at night, this master of the skies may have wrapped itself up in its wings and hung upside down from a branch, just like a bat.

How incredible a **Pterodactylus** must have looked in flight!

Some scientists think **Pterodactylus** may have had a throat pouch, much like a pelican's. This throat pouch may have been used for storing fish that it caught and then brought to its young.

In his book, *The Lost World*, Sir Arthur Conan Doyle imagines spotting some pterosaurs, which had survived from Jurassic times. *"It was a wonderful sight to see at least a hundred creatures of such enormous size and hideous appearance all swooping like swallows . . . above us."*

It would certainly have been kept busy, flying backward and forward to feed fledglings.

What were pterosaurs?

1

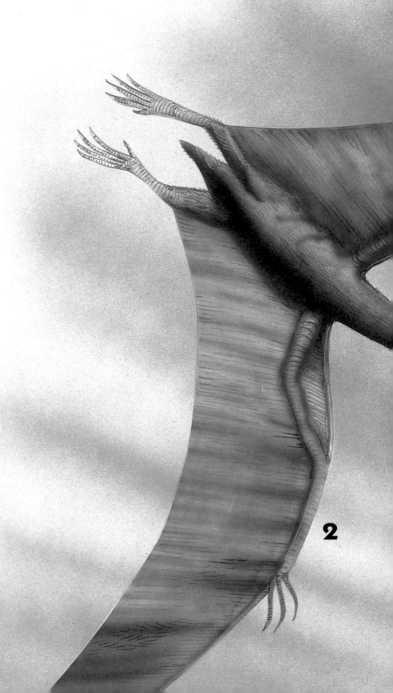

2

Dinosaurs ruled the Earth for 160 million years. Other creatures, meanwhile, ruled the skies. These were the pterosaurs, or winged reptiles.

Birds evolved after the pterosaurs. But, very surprisingly, scientists now know that birds did not evolve from these flying reptiles but from dinosaurs! In fact, the skeletons of early birds and the skeletons of some of their dinosaur relatives are very much alike.

Some pterosaurs were tiny, as small as a robin, or smaller. Others were the size of a small airplane. Some had strong muscles and could flap their wings to fly. Others had to rely on currents of air to help them glide along.

Scientists believe that, although dinosaurs and pterosaurs were different types of creatures, they had a common link in animals such as **Lagosuchus**.

There were two main types of pterosaurs. **Rhamphorhynchoids** (RAM-FOE-RIN-KOIDS) (**1**) – their name means "prow beaks" – had long jaws, sharp teeth, short necks, and lengthy tails, with fur covering their bodies to keep them warm. **Pterodactyloids** (TER-OH-DAK-TIL-OIDS) – their name means "winged fingers" – had shorter tails but longer necks and, again, sharp teeth. The largest was probably **Quetzalcoatlus** (KET-ZAL-COAT-LUS) (**2**), whose name means "feathered serpent." It may have been the biggest flying creature the world has ever seen.

The first pterosaurs lived about 230 million years ago in the Triassic Period. A number of scientists believe that **Pterodactylus** and its flying relatives evolved from early creatures such as **Lagosuchus** (LAY-GO-SOO-KUS) (**3**), whose name means "rabbit crocodile."

3

11

Pterodactylus discovered

Most remains of pterosaurs have been found near coastlines. This has led some scientists to believe that pterosaurs were like modern seabirds, staying close to the ocean. But others say that there were probably just as many pterosaurs that flew over land.

Pterodactylus was discovered long before any dinosaurs had been dug up. An Italian scientist named Cosmo Alessandro Collini found some remains in a quarry in southern Germany over two hundred years ago, in 1784. He was baffled by them at first and thought they belonged to a fishlike creature. Or had he found a bat or a type of bird?

It was not until many years later that the French scientist Georges Cuvier realized the bones came from a type of reptile. He saw that its fourth finger was very long and called the creature **Pterodactylus**, meaning "wing finger."

About 50 years after **Pterodactylus** had first been discovered, another scientist noticed something interesting.

Its bones had air passages running
through them, just like the bones
of modern birds. This seemed to
prove it was built for flight.
Gradually, it became clear
to scientists, though, that
Pterodactylus was
quite different from
any of today's
animals.

Three, two, one — liftoff!

What kind of flying creature was **Pterodactylus**? Scientists believe it must have been one of the best-equipped fliers of prehistoric times. They can tell, by examining marks on its bones, that **Pterodactylus** had strong muscles attached to its wings. This shows us that it could flap them quite powerfully.

One scientist who has studied **Pterodactylus** believes that, when tired, it rested upside down by hanging from its toes from a branch on a tree. All **Pterodactylus** would have needed to do to take off would have been to drop down, stretch its wings, and flap them. If **Pterodactylus** was on the ground and wanted to fly away, it would face the wind and spread its wings. One little jump and a flap of the wings, and it was airborne.

It is still not clear exactly how **Pterodactylus** moved when it was on the ground. But it could move around more easily than a bat, which can only crawl along on its tummy.

Some experts think **Pterodactylus** could walk upright on its back legs. Others think it would have shuffled along on all fours. But its forelimbs were more suited to climbing than to walking.

And what if **Pterodactylus** happened to land on water when fishing for food? There may have been webs between its toes, much like a duck's. If it spread its toes, the webs would help to make a sort of paddle so it could skim over the water. Then, **Pterodactylus** would probably use its feet to thrust itself up into the air.

15

Pterodactylus's day

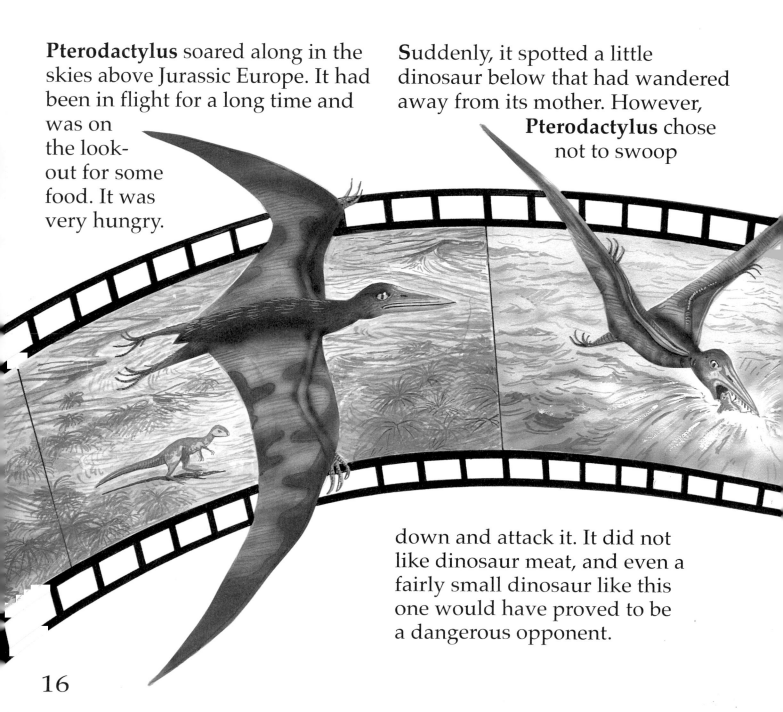

Pterodactylus soared along in the skies above Jurassic Europe. It had been in flight for a long time and was on the look-out for some food. It was very hungry.

Suddenly, it spotted a little dinosaur below that had wandered away from its mother. However, **Pterodactylus** chose not to swoop down and attack it. It did not like dinosaur meat, and even a fairly small dinosaur like this one would have proved to be a dangerous opponent.

Pterodactylus preferred to eat marine creatures.

It had a marvelous fishing technique, and when it saw a river up ahead, decided to go into action. **Pterodactylus** flew parallel with the water, opening its bottom jaw as it did so. Before long, it had a mouthful of tiny shrimps.

This giant marine reptile lifted its head above the surface of the water and snapped at **Pterodactylus**. The pterosaur was so surprised, it lost its balance and dropped the shrimps. This was not a safe place to go fishing!

The hungry pterosaur now decided to search for food another way. It rested on its front limbs and dug its beak into the earth.

But it had disturbed one of the monsters of the prehistoric deep – **Plesiosaurus** (<u>PLEES</u>-EE-OH-<u>SAW</u>-RUS).

It knew that there were plenty of crawling creatures just beneath the ground. If fish was not on the menu, worms would do!

Eggs and nests

Paleontologists (scientists who study the remains of animals) have never actually found any fossilized pterosaur eggs. But they agree that pterosaurs, such as **Pterodactylus**, must have given birth this way.

However, their bodies were not large enough to lay many eggs at once. Also, the females would not have been able to fly with several eggs in their bodies. The mothers, therefore, probably only laid one or two eggs at a time.

Pterodactylus would also have had to be careful about where they built their nests because some dinosaurs were egg thieves. They may have made nests in mountains.

Scientists think **Pterodactylus** brought food to its young and fed them. It did this by storing food in its throat. The baby would then put its beak into the adult's mouth to pick out a meal, piece by piece.

The parents may also have regurgitated food that they had eaten earlier, like birds do today.

Male and female **Pterodactylus** may even have paired for life, producing new young every year.

A fledgling **Pterodactylus** would have been very small when it was born. If the weather got cold, **Pterodactylus** parents would have been able to fold their wings around their babies to keep them warm. The babies grew quickly, however, and soon learned to fly.

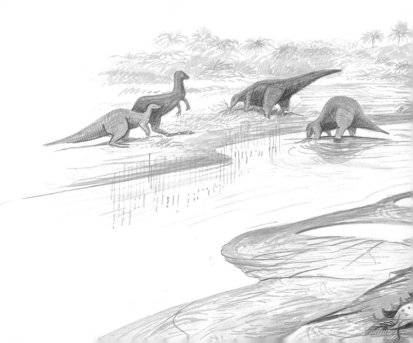

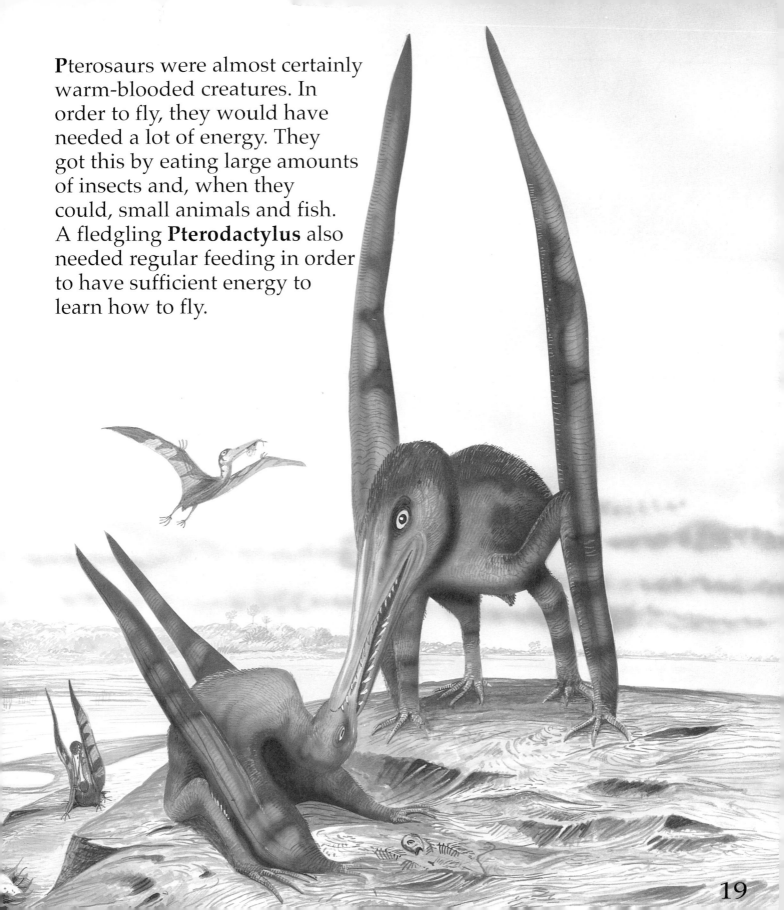

Pterosaurs were almost certainly
warm-blooded creatures. In
order to fly, they would have
needed a lot of energy. They
got this by eating large amounts
of insects and, when they
could, small animals and fish.
A fledgling **Pterodactylus** also
needed regular feeding in order
to have sufficient energy to
learn how to fly.

Pterodactylus data

Known for its short tail, **Pterodactylus** had several other features that would have made it easy to recognize in the sky if you had been around at the time. So let's imagine what it might have been like to go **Pterodactylus**-spotting!

Flying fingers

Pterodactylus has four fingers. The first three can be moved around, are used for holding or gripping, and have claws on the ends. The fourth finger is amazingly long and is attached to the wing.

Sharp teeth

Does the flying reptile have small, but sharp, teeth in both its upper and lower jaws? We are looking for teeth that curve outward and are especially well suited for cutting into fish.

Thin wing

Now look at its wingspan. The largest wingspan of any **Pterodactylus** is 8 feet (2.5 meters) — that's bigger than a fully grown adult human being. But some **Pterodactylus** are much smaller. As you can see, the wing consists of thin skin stretched between the long fourth finger and the lower part of the leg. **Pterodactylus** has to take great care that it does not tear this wing or damage the bones that hold it in place. Its wings are as thin as a rubber band and are made from a material not found in any modern animals.

Big brain

How intelligent does this flying reptile seem to be? For a creature of its size, **Pterodactylus** has a large brain that looks like the illustration shown here. It has to have a fairly advanced brain in order to cope successfully with flying, which is a complicated activity.

Size differences

Some **Pterodactylus** are much larger than others. **Pterodactylus antiquus**, for instance, has a skull about three times as big as the skull of **Pterodactylus elegans**. Apart from their size, however, they are very much alike.

Where in the world?

So far, scientists have discovered **Pterodactylus** in places as far apart as France, Africa, Germany, and England. But, of course, they may have existed elsewhere, and their skeletons may yet be found by paleontologists of the future. You may even come across one if you join a dig!

Pterodactylus and cousins

Pterodactylus (**1**) was a short-tailed **Pterodactyloid** that lived in the Late Jurassic Period, about 150 million years ago. Many other **Pterodactyloids** soared the Jurassic skies with **Pterodactylus**. Let's meet some of them.

Remains of **Germanodactylus** (GER-MAN-OH-DAK-TIL-US) (**2**) have been found in Germany and England. **Germanodactylus** had strong finger claws, sharp teeth, and a wingspan of up to 3 feet (1 m). Its name means "German finger." Unlike **Pterodactylus**, this pterosaur had a thin, bony crest on top of its head.

Gallodactylus (GAL-OH-DAK-TIL-US) (**3**) has a name meaning "Gallic finger" because it was first found in France. (*Gallic* means "from France.")

It looked like **Pterodactylus** in many ways, but it had a longer beak than most of its pterosaur cousins and teeth only in the front of its long, slender jaws. **Gallodactylus** also had a short crest at the back of its head. Its wingspan was about 4.5 feet (1.4 m).

Ctenochasma (TEN-OH-<u>KAZ</u>-MUH) (**4**) was discovered in 1862 in Germany. Its name means "comb jaw" because it had an amazing number of long, thin teeth that curved inward.

Scientists thought these teeth – there were 260 in one specimen – looked like those in a comb. **Ctenochasma** used its teeth to filter out unwanted bits when it was feeding. This pterosaur had a wingspan of about 4 feet (1.2 m).

These **Pterodactyloid** cousins were fascinating creatures!

GLOSSARY

fledglings — young birds.

forelimbs — front limbs, or parts of the body, such as arms, wings, or flippers.

fossils — traces or remains of plants and animals found in rock.

marine — living in or formed by the ocean or sea.

pouch — a baglike part, such as that on a pelican's bill, used to carry and store food.

quarry — a place where stone or marble is excavated, or dug up, from the ground.

regurgitate — to bring back up partly digested food from the stomach to the mouth.

remains — a skeleton, bones, or dead body.

reptiles — cold-blooded animals that have hornlike or scale-covered skin.

skeleton — the bony framework of a body.

INDEX